B

N

`GW01453008`

To

Happy Birthday

With love and best wishes from:

◇◇◇

1 January
The Soviet Union ceases to demand war reparations from West Germany.

1954 Birthday Notebook

◇◇

7 January
The first translation program (Russian to English) is used
with an IBM computer in New York.

◇◇

14 January
Marilyn Monroe marries baseball player Joe DiMaggio at
San Francisco City Hall.

_____

_____

_____

_____

_____

_____

_____

_____

_____

_____

_____

_____

_____

_____

21 January

The first nuclear powered submarine, the USS *Nautilus*, is launched in Groton, Connecticut by First Lady Mamie Eisenhower.

_____

_____

_____

_____

_____

_____

_____

_____

_____

_____

_____

_____

_____

_____

_____

_____

29 January
US talk show host Oprah Winfrey born in Kosciusko,
Mississippi.

◇◇

2 February

Elizabeth II, Queen of Australia, becomes the first reigning monarch to visit the country.

_____

_____

_____

_____

_____

_____

_____

_____

_____

_____

_____

_____

_____

_____

◇◇

10 February
President Dwight D. Eisenhower warns against US
intervention in Vietnam.

<><><><><><><><><><><><><><><><><><><><><><><><><><><><><><><><><>

18 February
Actor John Travolta born.

23 February

The first mass vaccination of children against polio begins in Pittsburgh, USA.

1954 Birthday Notebook

25 February
Lt Col Gamal Abdel Nasser becomes
Prime Minister of Egypt.

<><><><><><><><><><><><><><><><><><><><><><><><><><><><><><><>

1 March
The US government tests its new hydrogen bomb, on Bikini
Atoll in the Pacific Ocean. It is 1000 times more powerful
than the Hiroshima bomb.

_____

_____

_____

_____

_____

_____

_____

_____

_____

_____

_____

_____

_____

_____

_____

◇◇

13 March
The battle between French and Viet Minh troops begins at
Dien Bien Phu in Vietnam.

_____

_____

_____

_____

_____

_____

_____

_____

_____

_____

_____

_____

_____

_____

◇◇

19 March
Joey Giardello knocks out Willie Tory at Madison Square
Garden, the first boxing match to be televised in colour.

_____

_____

_____

_____

_____

_____

_____

_____

_____

_____

_____

_____

_____

_____

_____

25 March
From Here to Eternity starring Burt Lancaster and Deborah Kerr wins eight Academy Awards including Best Picture.

_____

_____

_____

_____

_____

_____

_____

_____

_____

_____

_____

_____

_____

_____

◇◇

30 March
Canada's first underground railway opens in Toronto.

_____

_____

_____

_____

_____

_____

_____

_____

_____

_____

_____

_____

_____

_____

◇◇◇

2 April
The Grove Family, Britain's first TV soap opera, is broadcast on the BBC.

4 April
Following a memory lapse during a live broadcast, legendary conductor Arturo Toscanini announces his retirement.

_____

_____

_____

_____

_____

_____

_____

_____

_____

_____

_____

_____

_____

_____

◇◇

7 April
Dwight D. Eisenhower gives a speech outlining his 'domino theory' of how countries fall under communism.

14 April

Aneurin Bevan resigns from the British Labour Party's shadow cabinet.

_____

_____

_____

_____

_____

_____

_____

_____

_____

_____

_____

_____

_____

_____

◇◇

22 April

Senator Joseph McCarthy begins investigating alleged
communist infiltration in the US army as part of his series of
'witch hunts'.

_____

_____

_____

_____

_____

_____

_____

_____

_____

_____

_____

_____

_____

_____

1954 Birthday Notebook

1 May
The Unification Church, known as the 'Moonies' is founded in South Korea.

6 May

Roger Bannister becomes the first man on record to run a
mile in under four minutes, in Oxford, England.

_____

_____

_____

_____

_____

_____

_____

_____

_____

_____

_____

_____

_____

_____

<><><><><><><><><><><><><><><><><><><><><><><><><><><>

7 May
After nearly two months of fighting against overwhelming
odds, French forces are defeated at Dien Bien Phu.

_____

_____

_____

_____

_____

_____

_____

_____

_____

_____

_____

_____

_____

_____

<><><><><><><><><><><><><><><><><><><><><><><><><><><><><><><><><>

14 May
The prototype of the Boeing 707 airliner, the *Dash 80* is
completed, first flying on 15 July.

_____

_____

_____

_____

_____

_____

_____

_____

_____

_____

_____

_____

_____

_____

_____

◇◇

15 May

The Latin Union for the defence and promotion of Romance languages (Italian, French, Spanish, Portuguese and Romanian) is formed in Madrid.

_____

_____

_____

_____

_____

_____

_____

_____

_____

_____

_____

_____

_____

_____

<><><><><><><><><><><><><><><><><><><><><><><><><><><><><><><><><><><><><>

17 May
In *Brown* v *Board of Education* the US Supreme Court rules
that racial segregation in schools is unconstitutional.

_____

_____

_____

_____

_____

_____

_____

_____

_____

_____

_____

_____

_____

_____

_____

<><><><><><><><><><><><><><><><><><><><><><><><><><><><><><>

20 May
Bill Haley and the Comets release what is generally
acknowledged to be the first rock and roll song, *Rock
Around the Clock.*

_____

_____

_____

_____

_____

_____

_____

_____

_____

_____

_____

_____

_____

_____

◇◇

29 May
Prince Bernhard of the Netherlands establishes the secretive
Bilderberg Group to promote dialogue between Europe and
North America.

_____

_____

_____

_____

_____

_____

_____

_____

_____

_____

_____

_____

_____

_____

◇◇

6 June
J.R.R. Tolkien's *The Lord of the Rings* is published.

_____

_____

_____

_____

_____

_____

_____

_____

_____

_____

_____

_____

_____

_____

_____

7 June
British computing pioneer Alan Turing OBE commits
suicide aged 41.

_____

_____

_____

_____

_____

_____

_____

_____

_____

_____

_____

_____

_____

_____

◇◇

14 June

The words 'under God' are added to the United State's Pledge of Allegiance.

_____

_____

_____

_____

_____

_____

_____

_____

_____

_____

_____

_____

_____

_____

_____

15 June
The Union of European Football Associations (UEFA) is formed in Basel, Switzerland.

27 June

The world's first atomic power station opens at Obninsk near Moscow.

_____

_____

_____

_____

_____

_____

_____

_____

_____

_____

_____

_____

_____

_____

_____

1954 Birthday Notebook

<><><><><><><><><><><><><><><><><><><><><><><><><>

4 July
Food rationing ends in Britain 14 years after it began during the Second World War.

_____

_____

_____

_____

_____

_____

_____

_____

_____

_____

_____

_____

_____

_____

◇◇

13 July
Mexican painter Frida Kahlo dies aged 47.

19 July
Elvis Presley releases his first single *That's All Right* in Memphis, Tennessee.

◇◇

31 July

Italian mountaineers Lino Lacedelli and Achille Compagnoni become the first climbers to reach the summit of K2, the second highest mountain in the world.

_____

_____

_____

_____

_____

_____

_____

_____

_____

_____

_____

_____

_____

_____

<><><><><><><><><><><><><><><><><><><><><><><><><><><><><><><><><><>

1 August
The First Indochina War ends with a defeat of French forces
by the Vietnamese.

_____

_____

_____

_____

_____

_____

_____

_____

_____

_____

_____

_____

_____

_____

_____

1954 Birthday Notebook

◇◇◇

4 August

The English Electric *Lightning* supersonic jet fighter flies for the first time.

◇◇◇

5 August
One of the longest running musicals in British theatre history, *Salad Days*, opens in London.

◇◇◇◇◇◇◇◇◇◇◇◇◇◇◇◇◇◇◇◇◇◇◇◇◇◇◇◇◇◇◇◇◇◇◇◇◇◇◇

16 August
The first issue of *Sports Illustrated* magazine is published in the USA.

◇◇

3 September
The last episode of the US radio serial *The Lone Ranger* is broadcast after 2956 episodes over 21 years.

◇◇

11 September
The first televised Miss America pageant is broadcast.

◇◇

17 September

William Golding's novel *The Lord of the Flies* is published in London.

_____

_____

_____

_____

_____

_____

_____

_____

_____

_____

_____

_____

_____

_____

_____

15 October
Hurricane Hazel hits the USA, the only recorded Category 4 hurricane to reach as far as North Carolina.

_____

_____

_____

_____

_____

_____

_____

_____

_____

_____

_____

_____

_____

_____

<<<<<<<<<<<<<<<<<<<<<<<<<<<<<<<<<<<<<<<<<<<<<<<<<<<<<<>

18 October

Texas Instruments develops the first commercial transistor radio, the Regency TR-1.

_____

_____

_____

_____

_____

_____

_____

_____

_____

_____

_____

_____

_____

_____

◇◇

31 October
The Algerian National Liberation Front begins an uprising against French colonial rule.

_____

_____

_____

_____

_____

_____

_____

_____

_____

_____

_____

_____

_____

_____

_____

<><><><><><><><><><><><><><><><><><><><><><><><><><><><><><><><>

2 November
Hit comedy *Hancock's Half Hour* starring Tony Hancock, Sid James and Hattie Jacques is first broadcast on BBC radio.

_____

_____

_____

_____

_____

_____

_____

_____

_____

_____

_____

_____

_____

_____

◇◇◇

3 November

The first *Godzilla* film premieres in Japan. It becomes the longest running franchise in film history.

_____

_____

_____

_____

_____

_____

_____

_____

_____

_____

_____

_____

_____

_____

_____

1954 Birthday Notebook

8 November
Nobel Prize winning author Sir Kazuo Ishiguro OBE
(*The Remains of the Day*) is born in Nagasaki, Japan.

_____

_____

_____

_____

_____

_____

_____

_____

_____

_____

_____

_____

_____

_____

3 November
French artist Henri Matisse dies aged 84.

1954 Birthday Notebook

◇◇

10 November

The USMC War Memorial (The 'Iwo Jima' memorial) is
dedicated at Arlington National Cemetery.

12 November
Ellis Island, the main immigration port of New York City, closes permanently.

_____

_____

_____

_____

_____

_____

_____

_____

_____

_____

_____

_____

_____

_____

◇◇

13 November

Great Britain defeats France in the first ever Rugby League
World Cup in Paris.

◇◇

30 November

The first recorded case of an object from outer space hitting a human takes place when a meteorite hits a woman in her home at Sylacauga, Alabama.

_____

_____

_____

_____

_____

_____

_____

_____

_____

_____

_____

_____

_____

_____

⟡⟡

1 December

The first Hyatt Hotel opens in Los Angeles; it is also the first
hotel to be built on airport property.

_____

_____

_____

_____

_____

_____

_____

_____

_____

_____

_____

_____

_____

1954 Birthday Notebook

◇◇◇

2 December
The US Senate condemns Senator Joseph McCarthy for his over-zealous investigations of communist infiltration.

4 December
The first Burger King restaurant opens in Miami, Florida.

23 December
J. Hartwell Harrison and Joseph Murray perform the first successful kidney transplant in Boston, Mass.

19605857R00036

Printed in Great Britain
by Amazon